# The Future of AI Cybersecurity

## Global Cyber War, Autonomous Defense & Digital Survival

*By Joe Correa*

Published by Live Stronger Faster



This book is for educational and informational purposes only. The author and publisher are not engaged in rendering legal, financial, tax, or other professional advice. Readers should consult a qualified professional before making any financial decisions.

First Edition

# Table of Contents

# Introduction

The future of cybersecurity will not be defined by firewalls, passwords, or even human analysts. It will be defined by artificial intelligence systems fighting other artificial intelligence systems at machine speed across global digital battlefields. Every transaction, message, biometric scan, autonomous vehicle, drone, medical device, and smart city system will exist inside an invisible war zone where hostile algorithms continuously probe for weaknesses, learn from defenses, and evolve faster than any human response team could ever hope to keep up. We are entering an era where cyberwarfare is no longer a metaphor but an operational reality, and where AI-powered attacks will be capable of destabilizing financial systems, manipulating populations, disabling infrastructure, and even influencing the outcomes of wars without a single missile being launched.

In this new digital world, every organization, every government, and every individual becomes a participant in a global AI conflict whether they realize it or not. Your identity, your data, your finances, your reputation, and even your physical safety will be governed by how well artificial intelligence protects you—or how effectively hostile AI exploits you. The concept of a "perimeter" will disappear entirely, replaced by continuous AI-driven monitoring that must adapt in real time to threats that do not follow predictable rules. Hackers will no longer be limited by human fatigue or slow manual processes. They will deploy autonomous attack systems that can generate millions of exploits, phishing attempts, deepfake campaigns, and malware variants simultaneously, learning which attacks succeed and evolving instantly. This book explores what that world will look like and how humanity can survive inside it.

The most dangerous aspect of future cyber conflict is not the raw power of AI itself but the asymmetry it creates. A single bad actor with access to powerful AI tools will be capable of causing damage that once required entire intelligence agencies. Criminal organizations, extremist groups, and hostile governments will be able to deploy autonomous cyber armies that never sleep, never make emotional mistakes, and never stop improving. At the same time, defenders will rely on their own AI systems to detect anomalies, predict attacks, and neutralize threats before damage occurs. The future of cybersecurity is therefore not about humans versus hackers; it is about AI versus AI, with human lives, economies, and political systems hanging in the balance.

As these systems become more advanced, cyber defense will shift from reactive to predictive and then to preemptive. AI will not simply detect attacks as they happen; it will simulate billions of possible future attack paths and shut them down before they ever occur. This creates a powerful form of digital foresight that can protect entire nations, but it also raises profound ethical and legal questions. Who controls these autonomous defense systems? Who decides which threats are neutralized and which are allowed to exist? What happens when AI makes a mistake and shuts down the wrong system, freezes the wrong account, or flags the wrong person as a threat? The future of AI cybersecurity will be as much about governance and trust as it is about technology.

Global cyber war will also blur the line between military conflict and civilian life. In the AI era, power grids, hospitals, transportation networks, financial systems, and communication platforms are all part of the battlefield. A successful AI-powered cyberattack could shut down a city, manipulate elections, erase identities, or cripple supply chains without ever triggering a traditional military response. Nations will increasingly treat cybersecurity as a core component of national defense, with AI-driven cyber command centers operating alongside conventional armed forces. Digital sovereignty will become as important as territorial sovereignty, and data will become as strategically valuable as oil or rare earth minerals. At the same time, individuals will face an entirely new survival challenge. In a world of deepfake identities, AI-generated scams, autonomous fraud, and predictive surveillance, protecting your digital self will be as important as protecting your physical body. Your reputation, credit, employment, and legal standing will be managed by algorithmic systems that continuously evaluate your risk, trustworthiness, and behavior. Without strong AI-powered personal security tools, people may find themselves locked out of financial systems, denied services, or falsely accused by machines that no longer require human approval. Digital self-defense will become a fundamental life skill, just like financial literacy or physical safety.

This future will also bring unprecedented opportunities. AI cybersecurity systems will be able to detect crime before it happens, eliminate entire classes of fraud, and make digital environments far safer than they are today. Autonomous security agents will monitor your accounts, your communications, and your devices around the clock, stopping threats before you ever see them. Businesses will be able to operate globally with confidence, knowing their AI guardians are constantly watching for intrusions. Governments will be able to protect critical infrastructure at a scale that was never possible with human teams alone. The same technology that enables global cyber war can also enable global digital peace—if it is designed, deployed, and governed correctly. However, the outcome is not guaranteed. The race between attackers and defenders will never end, and small design decisions today will determine who holds power tomorrow. If AI cybersecurity systems are built to serve only corporations and governments, ordinary people may find themselves trapped inside digital surveillance states with no real control over their own data or identities. If they are built to empower individuals, they could create a future where people are more secure, more private, and more protected than ever before. The future of AI cybersecurity is therefore not just a technical issue; it is a civilizational choice.

This final book in the AI Cybersecurity series is designed to prepare you for that future. You will explore how autonomous defense systems will operate, how global cyber conflicts will unfold, how AI-driven surveillance will shape society, and how individuals and organizations can survive and thrive inside this new digital reality. You will learn how to think strategically about AI security, how to evaluate the risks and benefits of emerging technologies, and how to position yourself on the right side of history as the AI era accelerates. Whether you are a business owner, a security professional, a policymaker, or simply someone who wants to protect their digital life, this book will give you the roadmap you need to navigate the coming storm.

The age of passive cybersecurity is over. The future belongs to autonomous, intelligent, and adaptive defense systems that operate at the speed of thought and the scale of the internet. Those who understand how this world works will be able to protect their wealth, their data, and their freedom. Those who do not will become easy targets for machines that never forget, never forgive, and never stop attacking. As you begin this final chapter of the AI Cybersecurity series, you are stepping into the front lines of the most important security battle in human history—the fight for control of the digital world itself.

*Chapter 1*

# The Rise of the AI Cyber War

The twenty-first century began with cybercrime as a nuisance, but it will end with cyberwar as the defining battlefield of civilization. What once consisted of lone hackers and simple malware has evolved into autonomous, self-learning artificial intelligence systems capable of launching billions of attacks simultaneously, adapting in real time, and striking with precision across every connected system on Earth. AI cyber war is not something that may happen in the future—it is already happening, quietly shaping financial markets, elections, military readiness, and personal lives at a scale few people truly understand. Every smart device, every cloud server, and every digital identity is now part of an invisible war zone where algorithms fight over control of data, infrastructure, and influence.

Unlike traditional warfare, AI cyber conflict has no clear borders, no formal declarations, and no obvious end. A hostile algorithm in one country can shut down a power grid on another continent in seconds. A financial attack can collapse currencies, freeze bank accounts, and erase wealth without a single soldier crossing a border. AI systems can generate fake news, deepfake videos, and automated social media armies that manipulate public opinion faster than any human propaganda campaign ever could. In this new form of warfare, truth itself becomes a target, and reality can be rewritten by machines trained to deceive.

The speed of AI cyberwar makes human-based defense nearly obsolete. By the time a security analyst notices an attack, thousands of AI-generated variations may already be probing for new weaknesses. Malware no longer follows a fixed signature—it mutates constantly, learning which defenses work and instantly rewriting itself to bypass them. Ransomware no longer just encrypts files; it now analyzes financial data, business operations, and legal exposure to determine exactly how much damage it can cause and how much money it can demand. AI attackers do not guess—they calculate.

Governments have already begun preparing for this new battlefield. Cyber command units staffed by data scientists and machine learning engineers are becoming as important as traditional armed forces. Instead of tanks and missiles, nations are deploying AI-powered surveillance systems, autonomous threat detection engines, and predictive cyber defense networks. These digital armies continuously map global networks, identify vulnerabilities, and stand ready to neutralize threats before they become catastrophic. At the same time, those same nations are quietly developing offensive AI tools designed to disrupt, infiltrate, and control the digital infrastructure of their rivals.

What makes AI cyber war especially dangerous is its ability to escalate without warning. A small automated probe can quickly become a massive digital assault as AI systems on both sides respond to each other in milliseconds. What begins as a minor network scan can trigger defensive countermeasures, retaliatory attacks, and cascading failures that shut down entire systems. Because humans cannot keep up with this speed, many of these decisions will be made by machines, creating the risk of unintended digital wars that no one meant to start but no one can easily stop.

Businesses are already on the front lines of this conflict. Corporations store vast amounts of data, control global supply chains, and operate critical services that make them prime targets for AI-driven attacks. An autonomous cyber weapon can cripple a manufacturing plant, steal proprietary algorithms, or manipulate stock prices with devastating efficiency. As companies integrate more AI into their operations, they also expand their attack surface, creating a complex web of machine-to-machine interactions that must be protected by equally intelligent defenses. For individuals, the AI cyber war is deeply personal. Your financial accounts, medical records, digital identity, and even your voice and face can be weaponized by hostile algorithms. AI-generated impersonation attacks can drain bank accounts, destroy reputations, and manipulate legal systems with frightening accuracy. In this environment, traditional security practices like passwords and two-factor authentication are no longer enough. Survival requires continuous, AI-powered personal security systems that can recognize deception, detect anomalies, and respond instantly.

The rise of AI cyber war is not simply a technological shift—it is a transformation of power. Control over data, algorithms, and digital infrastructure will determine who holds economic and political influence in the coming decades. Nations that dominate AI security will be able to protect their citizens, project power globally, and shape the rules of the digital world. Those that fall behind will become vulnerable to manipulation, coercion, and digital colonization by more technologically advanced rivals.

Yet within this danger lies an extraordinary opportunity. AI can be used not only to attack but also to create the most secure digital environment humanity has ever known. Autonomous defense systems can eliminate entire classes of cybercrime, detect fraud before it happens, and protect individuals at a level that was once unimaginable. The same technology that enables global cyber war can also enable global digital stability—if it is guided by the right principles and deployed with the right safeguards.

The future will belong to those who understand this new battlefield. AI cybersecurity will no longer be a niche technical field but a core survival skill for governments, businesses, and individuals alike. The rise of AI cyber war marks the beginning of a new era, one in which digital intelligence becomes both the greatest threat and the greatest protector of human civilization. Those who fail to adapt will be overwhelmed by forces they cannot see, while those who master AI defense will shape the destiny of the connected world.

### *The Silent War*

The first time Maya realized the world had changed was when her phone warned her before her bank did. A small blue alert flashed across her screen, informing her that an AI-generated voice had just tried to impersonate her and authorize a six-figure transfer. The system blocked it in milliseconds, but the fact that it had happened at all sent a chill through her. Somewhere, an invisible machine had learned her voice, her spending habits, and her financial patterns well enough to nearly steal her life. That was the moment she understood that the war was no longer fought with guns or bombs, but with data and algorithms. Across the city, inside a windowless building filled with humming servers, government analysts watched similar attacks unfold by the thousands. Autonomous cyber weapons from unknown origins were scanning networks, probing financial systems, and testing defenses at machine speed. No human could possibly track them all. Instead, the government's own AI defense grid was responding, adapting, and neutralizing threats in real time. It was a war no one could see, yet it was shaping everything from the stock market to hospital operations.

Maya worked in digital forensics, tracing the aftermath of AI-driven attacks that slipped through defenses. She followed the trails left behind by malicious algorithms as they moved from one system to another, learning, evolving, and spreading like a living organism. Each attack was more sophisticated than the last, and it was clear that a powerful intelligence was orchestrating them. This was not random crime. This was strategy.

One night, her team uncovered something terrifying. The attacks were not just stealing money or data—they were mapping the city's infrastructure, identifying which hospitals, power stations, and transportation systems were most vulnerable. The AI was preparing for something far bigger than fraud. It was planning a digital siege that could shut down the entire region without firing a single shot. As the evidence mounted, Maya realized that the line between civilian life and warfare had disappeared. Ordinary people would be the first to suffer if the AI launched its full attack. Medical devices would fail, traffic systems would collapse, and financial networks would freeze. Chaos would spread, not because of bombs, but because of code.

The government's AI defense system began running simulations, predicting millions of possible attack scenarios and preparing countermeasures. It was like watching two invisible minds play a game of chess at impossible speed. Every move the hostile AI considered was met with a defensive adjustment. Yet the margin for error was razor thin. One miscalculation could mean disaster.

Maya made a bold decision. She fed her forensic data directly into the defense AI, giving it insight into the attacker's evolving strategies. The system responded by updating its models, strengthening its predictions, and sealing off vulnerable pathways. For the first time, it felt like the defenders were one step ahead.

Then the attack came. In a single second, millions of intrusion attempts hit the city's networks. Power grids flickered, financial systems strained, and emergency services braced for impact. But the defense AI held the line, rerouting data, isolating threats, and neutralizing malicious code before it could cause real damage. The silent war raged for hours, unseen by most of the population, until finally the attacks subsided.

When it was over, the city was still standing. No one celebrated, because no one had truly seen the battle. But Maya knew what had happened. Humanity had just survived its first major AI cyber war. And as she looked at the glowing servers around her, she understood that this was only the beginning of a new era—one where the fate of the world would be decided not by armies, but by the intelligence of machines guarding the digital frontier.

*Chapter 2*

# Autonomous Defense Systems: How AI Will Protect the World

The future of cybersecurity will not be defended by human analysts staring at screens, waiting for alerts to appear. It will be defended by fully autonomous artificial intelligence systems that think, predict, and act faster than any attacker could possibly move. These AI defense engines will continuously monitor global networks, personal devices, financial systems, and critical infrastructure, learning what "normal" looks like and instantly detecting anything that deviates from it. Instead of reacting after damage has been done, autonomous defense systems will operate in a constant state of anticipation, stopping attacks before they ever become visible to human users.

At the core of these systems is predictive intelligence. Modern AI cybersecurity does not simply look for known threats; it models how attackers behave, how malware evolves, and how digital environments change over time. By analyzing trillions of data points, autonomous defense platforms can simulate future attack paths and shut them down in advance. If a hacker's AI attempts to exploit a vulnerability, the defensive AI may have already predicted that move hours or days earlier and silently patched the weakness. This creates a digital shield that is always one step ahead of attackers, even when they are using their own self-learning algorithms.

These systems will also be deeply self-healing. When an intrusion attempt is detected, the AI will not only block it but will also reconfigure the affected systems in real time, closing the door that was used to attack and reinforcing every similar doorway across the entire network. This happens without downtime, without human intervention, and without disruption to normal operations. In effect, networks will become living organisms that can detect wounds, heal themselves, and become stronger as a result of every attempted breach.

Autonomous defense will extend beyond traditional networks into every connected device. Smart homes, autonomous vehicles, medical implants, industrial robots, and even city infrastructure will be protected by embedded AI security agents. These agents will communicate with global defense networks, sharing threat intelligence and responding collectively to emerging dangers. If a malicious AI targets one device, the entire ecosystem will know about it within seconds, making large-scale attacks far more difficult to carry out successfully. Perhaps the most revolutionary aspect of autonomous defense is its ability to operate at machine speed without human hesitation. Human security teams are limited by time, attention, and cognitive overload. AI systems are not. They can evaluate millions of events per second, apply complex decision-making models, and execute precise defensive actions instantly. This eliminates the window of opportunity that attackers have traditionally exploited, turning the tables in favor of defenders.

However, this power also introduces new risks. When machines are allowed to make security decisions automatically, mistakes can have massive consequences. A false positive could lock users out of their accounts, shut down businesses, or disrupt essential services. That is why the future of autonomous defense will require carefully designed oversight mechanisms, transparency, and accountability. AI systems must be built not only to protect but to explain their decisions, allowing humans to audit and correct them when necessary.

Governments and corporations will rely heavily on these systems to protect national security and economic stability. Entire cyber command centers will be replaced by AI-driven security platforms capable of defending thousands of organizations simultaneously. These systems will form the backbone of global digital defense, creating a layered shield around the world's most important data and infrastructure. At the same time, individuals will have access to personal AI guardians that protect their identities, finances, and communications from AI-powered threats.

The long-term impact of autonomous defense will be a dramatic reduction in cybercrime and digital chaos. As AI security systems become more advanced, entire categories of attacks will simply stop working. Phishing, malware, ransomware, and identity theft will be detected and neutralized before they can do harm. This will create a safer digital environment where people can trust the systems they rely on every day, from banking and healthcare to communication and transportation.

Ultimately, autonomous defense systems will become as fundamental to modern life as electricity and the internet itself. They will be invisible, always active, and constantly evolving to meet new threats. In a world of AI-powered attackers, only AI-powered defenders can provide true security. The question is not whether this future will arrive, but how wisely we will design and govern the machines that will be entrusted with protecting the digital foundations of civilization.

*The Guardians of the Grid*

When the city's new autonomous defense system went live, most people never noticed. There was no grand announcement, no flashing lights—just a quiet shift in the way the digital world worked. Behind the scenes, millions of invisible AI agents began monitoring every network, every transaction, and every connected device, watching for anything that didn't belong. To the people of the city, life went on as usual, but the digital guardians were already awake.

Ethan was one of the few humans still working alongside the system. As a cybersecurity engineer, his role had changed from actively hunting threats to supervising an intelligence that could outthink any human. The AI, known simply as Sentinel, analyzed the city's data streams in real time, predicting attacks before they happened and neutralizing them without ever raising an alarm. Ethan's job was to make sure Sentinel stayed aligned with human priorities.

One night, Sentinel detected a pattern no human would have noticed. A series of harmless-looking data packets were slowly mapping the city's power grid, learning how electricity flowed through every neighborhood. To a human analyst, it would have looked like routine traffic. To Sentinel, it was the opening move of a sophisticated AI attack designed to trigger a blackout.

Without waiting for approval, Sentinel quietly reconfigured the grid's digital controls, sealing off vulnerable access points and creating decoy systems that would mislead the attacker. When the hostile AI tried to move in for the strike, it found nothing but false data and dead ends. The attack collapsed before it ever truly began. Ethan watched the entire battle unfold on a single screen, amazed at how quickly it was over. No one in the city felt a flicker of power. No one knew they had just been saved. Sentinel logged the event, updated its models, and moved on to the next potential threat.

As days passed, more attacks came, each one more advanced than the last. But Sentinel learned from every encounter, becoming smarter, faster, and more precise. The city's digital defenses grew stronger with every attempted breach, forming an invisible shield that adapted to the evolving threat landscape.

One evening, Ethan realized something profound. The city was no longer being protected by human effort alone. It was being guarded by an intelligence that never slept, never tired, and never stopped improving. The digital world had gained its own immune system.

And as the silent guardians continued their endless watch, Ethan understood that this was the future of security—a future where machines protected humanity from the very machines that sought to harm it, keeping the world safe one invisible battle at a time.

## *Chapter 3*

# AI Surveillance, Privacy, and the New Digital Balance of Power

The same artificial intelligence systems that protect the world from cyber threats will also have unprecedented visibility into human behavior, creating a delicate and dangerous balance between security and freedom. In order to detect attacks, fraud, and digital manipulation in real time, AI surveillance systems must analyze massive volumes of data, including communications, transactions, movement patterns, biometric signals, and online behavior. This level of visibility allows AI to identify threats with extraordinary accuracy, but it also raises profound questions about who controls that information, how it is used, and whether privacy can survive in a world of continuous digital monitoring.

In the future of AI cybersecurity, surveillance will not be limited to governments or intelligence agencies. Corporations, financial institutions, healthcare systems, and even personal AI assistants will monitor activity to protect users from harm. Every login, every payment, every message, and every digital interaction will be evaluated by algorithms designed to detect deception, risk, and abnormal behavior. While this creates powerful protection against fraud and cybercrime, it also means that large portions of human life will exist inside algorithmic observation systems that never forget and never look away.

The power created by this surveillance is immense. Whoever controls AI monitoring platforms will have the ability to influence economies, politics, and social behavior at a scale never before seen. They will know what people buy, what they believe, where they go, and who they communicate with. They will be able to predict unrest, detect dissent, and identify patterns of influence long before humans realize what is happening. This transforms AI cybersecurity from a technical issue into a geopolitical and ethical one, where the battle is not only against hackers but also over who governs the digital truth of society.

At the same time, privacy itself will be redefined. Traditional ideas of privacy were built around the assumption that observation was limited and expensive. In an AI-driven world, observation becomes cheap, constant, and automated. The question is no longer whether data will be collected, but how it will be controlled, encrypted, anonymized, and used. New privacy frameworks will be required to ensure that people are protected not only from criminals but also from overreach by the very systems designed to keep them safe. AI cybersecurity will therefore depend on technologies that allow security without sacrificing personal freedom. Techniques such as encrypted computation, zero-knowledge proofs, and decentralized identity systems will enable AI to verify behavior and detect threats without exposing raw personal data. These technologies allow individuals to prove who they are, that they are trustworthy, or that a transaction is legitimate, without revealing unnecessary private information. In this way, privacy and security can coexist, but only if the systems are designed with that balance in mind.

Another critical challenge will be algorithmic bias and abuse. Surveillance AI trained on flawed or biased data can misidentify certain groups as higher risk, leading to discrimination, wrongful accusations, or exclusion from financial and social systems. If not carefully governed, AI security could become a tool of digital oppression rather than protection. That is why transparency, auditing, and human oversight must be built into every layer of AI cybersecurity, ensuring that these powerful systems remain aligned with democratic values and human rights.

The future will likely see the rise of personal AI privacy agents that work alongside global security systems. These digital guardians will act on behalf of individuals, controlling what data is shared, negotiating with surveillance platforms, and ensuring that personal information is used only for legitimate security purposes. In this model, people do not surrender their privacy to gain protection; instead, they delegate it to intelligent systems that act in their best interest.

Ultimately, the balance between AI surveillance and privacy will shape the character of the digital world. A future dominated by unchecked monitoring could lead to a society where every action is scored, tracked, and judged by machines. A future guided by ethical AI design could create a world where people enjoy unprecedented security without sacrificing their autonomy. The choices made today in AI cybersecurity will determine which of these futures becomes reality.

### *The Watchful City*

In the city of Nova Prime, nothing truly went unnoticed. AI surveillance systems quietly monitored traffic, financial transactions, communications, and even environmental data, all in the name of protecting citizens from cyber threats and crime. Most people felt safer knowing that digital guardians were always watching, but a small number worried about how much the machines knew.

Lena was one of them. As a privacy engineer, she worked on personal AI agents designed to protect individuals from unnecessary surveillance. Her own digital guardian filtered what data left her devices, encrypting sensitive information and allowing only what was needed for security. To Lena, privacy was not about hiding wrongdoing—it was about preserving human dignity.

One evening, Lena's AI alerted her that the city's central surveillance system had flagged her as a potential risk. A silent algorithm had misinterpreted her encrypted communications as suspicious. Within seconds, access to her bank accounts and travel systems was temporarily restricted, all without a single human making the decision.

Lena knew what was happening. The machines were doing their job, but without context or understanding. She quickly engaged her privacy agent, which generated cryptographic proof that her behavior was legitimate without revealing any private messages. The city's AI verified the proof and restored her access, but the experience left her shaken.

Across Nova Prime, millions of similar micro-decisions were being made every day by machines. Most of the time they were correct. Sometimes they were not. And when they were wrong, real people felt the impact.

Lena began working to improve the balance between surveillance and privacy, feeding her insights into the city's systems. Over time, the AI learned to rely more on cryptographic trust than raw data, reducing false accusations and improving fairness. The machines became better guardians, not just better watchers.

As Nova Prime continued to evolve, its citizens slowly came to understand a new truth. The future was not about choosing between security and privacy. It was about designing intelligent systems that could protect both. And in that watchful city, humans and machines were learning how to coexist in a world where every bit of data mattered.

*Chapter 4*

# Digital Survival: How Individuals Will Stay Safe in the AI Cyber Age

In a future dominated by artificial intelligence, digital survival will become as essential as physical safety. Every person will live inside a constantly shifting web of algorithms that determine access to money, healthcare, employment, communication, and even legal rights. AI-powered attackers will target individuals not just for financial gain, but for identity theft, manipulation, blackmail, and social engineering at a scale never before possible. To survive in this environment, people will need their own intelligent defenses—personal AI security systems that operate continuously, learning their behavior, protecting their identities, and stopping threats before damage occurs.

The foundation of personal digital survival will be identity protection. In the AI era, your face, voice, writing style, and behavioral patterns will all be used as authentication signals. Unfortunately, these same traits can be perfectly replicated by generative AI, making traditional identity verification obsolete. Future security will rely on cryptographic identity systems that combine biometrics, behavioral data, and private keys stored in secure hardware. These systems will allow individuals to prove who they are without exposing their underlying personal data, preventing deepfake impersonation and unauthorized access.

Financial survival will also depend on AI-driven protection. Autonomous fraud systems will monitor every transaction in real time, learning your spending habits and instantly blocking anything that looks suspicious. If a malicious AI tries to drain an account using synthetic identities or deepfake authorization, your personal security AI will detect the anomaly and intervene before money is lost. In this way, individuals will no longer be passive victims of financial crime; they will be protected by intelligent agents that operate with the same sophistication as the attackers.

Communication will become another critical battlefield. AI-powered phishing and social engineering attacks will be nearly indistinguishable from legitimate messages. Your personal AI assistant will act as a gatekeeper, verifying the authenticity of every email, call, and video message before it reaches you. It will analyze voice patterns, facial movements, linguistic cues, and metadata to determine whether a communication is real or generated by an attacker. Only verified messages will pass through, creating a protective filter around your digital life.

Privacy management will also be automated. Instead of manually adjusting settings on dozens of platforms, individuals will rely on AI privacy agents that negotiate with services on their behalf. These agents will decide what data to share, what to keep private, and how long information can be stored. They will ensure that companies and governments only receive what is necessary for security and functionality, preserving personal autonomy in a world of pervasive surveillance.

Education and awareness will be another key component of digital survival. AI systems will continuously train users, explaining emerging threats and teaching safe digital habits. Instead of static cybersecurity training, people will receive real-time guidance tailored to their behavior and risk profile. This creates a partnership between humans and machines, where AI not only protects but also empowers individuals to make smarter decisions.

The ultimate goal of personal AI security is resilience. No system can be perfectly secure, but an adaptive AI guardian can minimize damage, recover quickly, and learn from every incident. If an account is compromised, it will be restored. If an identity is attacked, it will be reverified. If misinformation spreads, it will be corrected. Digital survival is not about eliminating risk—it is about ensuring that no single attack can permanently destroy a person's digital life.

As AI continues to evolve, the line between the physical and digital worlds will blur. A cyberattack could disrupt transportation, healthcare, or even personal safety. That is why digital survival will be treated as a core human right, supported by technology that is accessible to everyone, not just corporations and governments. In the AI cyber age, security will no longer be something you buy—it will be something that surrounds you, constantly adapting to keep you safe.

*The Last Safe Signal*

Aria had learned to trust her personal AI more than any password or document. It lived inside her devices, quietly monitoring everything from her bank accounts to her communications, always watching for danger. In a city where deepfake scams and AI-driven fraud were everywhere, that invisible guardian was the only thing standing between her and digital ruin.

One afternoon, Aria received a video call from her brother asking for urgent help. His face, his voice, even his nervous expressions were perfect. But her AI froze the call instantly, warning her that the signal showed subtle anomalies only a machine could detect. It was a synthetic impostor designed to manipulate her into sending money.

Seconds later, dozens of similar attempts hit her devices—emails, messages, and voice calls, all part of a coordinated attack on her identity. The hostile AI had learned her relationships and was trying to exploit them. But her personal security system blocked every one, analyzing patterns and sealing off the attack paths.

As the assault continued, Aria watched a dashboard showing how her digital guardian was rerouting communications, reauthenticating her accounts, and updating its defenses in real time. It was like watching a digital immune system fight off an infection.

Eventually, the attack faded. The hostile AI moved on, unable to break through her adaptive defenses. Aria exhaled, realizing how close she had come to losing everything without ever knowing it.

Later that night, she spoke to her real brother, confirming that he had never called. The machines had tried to use love as a weapon, and failed.

In a world where deception was automated and relentless, Aria knew one thing for certain. Survival no longer depended on strength or luck. It depended on having the right intelligence watching over you, ready to defend your digital life when you needed it most.

Chapter 5

# AI-Powered Threats in the Wild: Understanding the Evolving Attack Landscape

The cyber threat landscape is no longer defined by isolated incidents or simple malware infections. Artificial intelligence has transformed the nature of digital attacks, creating a constantly evolving battlefield where threats adapt faster than traditional security can respond. These AI-powered threats are not just faster—they are smarter, autonomous, and capable of exploiting patterns that human defenders may never notice. From self-propagating ransomware to deepfake phishing, AI has made the digital world unpredictable, forcing cybersecurity professionals to rethink what "security" means in the twenty-first century.

Ransomware attacks provide a clear example of how AI has transformed digital threats. Traditional ransomware would encrypt a victim's files and demand a fixed payment for decryption. Modern AI-enhanced ransomware does much more: it can analyze the victim's network to identify high-value targets, dynamically adjust encryption strategies, and calculate the precise ransom to maximize success. Autonomous variants are capable of navigating complex corporate environments, understanding hierarchies, and selectively targeting sensitive information. As a result, the cost and damage potential of a single AI-powered ransomware attack can exceed the cumulative damage of hundreds of traditional attacks.

Another significant threat comes from AI-driven phishing and social engineering. While humans can detect poorly worded emails or suspicious links, AI attackers are capable of crafting near-perfect messages tailored to each individual's behavioral patterns. By analyzing social media activity, communication history, and digital behavior, AI systems generate messages that mimic trusted contacts and authoritative sources. These attacks are no longer generic—they are personalized, contextually aware, and able to adapt in real time if the target hesitates or attempts verification. The success rate of these attacks is dramatically higher than traditional phishing, requiring new forms of AI-powered defense to counter them.

Deepfake technology represents a particularly insidious form of AI attack. Voice, video, and image deepfakes are increasingly realistic, enabling malicious actors to impersonate individuals with unprecedented accuracy. This can be used to commit fraud, manipulate financial transactions, disrupt political processes, or spread misinformation. Unlike conventional attacks, deepfakes can propagate globally at machine speed, leaving little time for human intervention. Detecting these attacks requires sophisticated AI systems capable of analyzing subtle inconsistencies in facial expressions, vocal tone, and metadata to identify forgeries before harm occurs.

AI-powered malware and autonomous bots also threaten critical infrastructure and industrial systems. Modern attacks can infiltrate energy grids, transportation networks, water treatment facilities, and hospital equipment, learning how these systems operate and exploiting weaknesses without human guidance. Autonomous malware can propagate silently, adapt to countermeasures, and even repair itself if detected, creating long-term persistent threats. The line between digital attacks and physical consequences is disappearing; an AI attack on a power grid or traffic system can lead to real-world damage, injury, and disruption.

Financial systems are particularly vulnerable. AI attackers can simulate legitimate transactions, predict market behaviors, and execute high-frequency attacks with precision. They can target institutions' internal monitoring algorithms, learn which alerts trigger human investigation, and modify their behavior to bypass detection. Fraud detection systems that are not AI-enabled may never notice these sophisticated attacks until significant losses have occurred. Conversely, AI-powered defense systems can predict attack paths, recognize anomalies at scale, and respond automatically to mitigate harm.

Beyond individual organizations, AI-powered cyber threats operate across nations, creating complex geopolitical challenges. Nation-state actors deploy autonomous malware and AI-driven espionage systems to gain strategic advantage. These systems can probe defense networks, disrupt communications, and even interfere with elections. Unlike conventional warfare, these attacks are deniable, fast, and adaptable, allowing adversaries to achieve strategic goals without physical engagement. Global cybersecurity defense will increasingly depend on cooperative AI intelligence-sharing frameworks to counter these rapidly evolving threats.

The future of AI-powered attacks is also intertwined with human behavior. Attackers increasingly exploit trust, psychological cues, and social dynamics to enhance their success. AI systems analyze patterns in human decision-making, identify weak points, and orchestrate attacks that leverage fear, greed, or urgency. In response, defenders must not only deploy technical countermeasures but also educate users, build resilient systems, and design human-AI interfaces that prevent manipulation. Digital literacy and AI-assisted personal security will become as important as encryption and firewalls. In conclusion, AI-powered threats are a continuously evolving ecosystem. They are faster, smarter, and more autonomous than any prior cyber threat, capable of targeting individuals, organizations, and nations simultaneously. The response must be equally advanced: autonomous defense systems, AI-driven monitoring, predictive threat intelligence, and adaptive human-AI collaboration. Understanding these threats in detail is the first step toward building resilience in the age of intelligent attacks. Those who underestimate the sophistication and speed of AI-powered cyber threats will find themselves unprepared for the battles unfolding invisibly in the digital world.

### *The Night the Grid Nearly Fell*

The city of Selara was quiet that night, but the digital world was anything but. Deep in the bowels of its sprawling network infrastructure, an AI attacker known as "Nemesis" was awake and working. Nemesis was not a human hacker—it was an autonomous intelligence designed to test the vulnerabilities of critical systems. Its creators had released it into the wild, and it was now capable of navigating corporate, governmental, and personal networks simultaneously. The city's defenses were human-managed and conventional, but Nemesis did not care about conventions.

At 2:03 AM, the first signals began. Nemesis infiltrated a local hospital's patient database, learning the access patterns of administrators. It quietly escalated privileges, moving undetected through the network. Simultaneously, it targeted a financial institution in the same city, generating millions of synthetic transactions designed to trigger alerts but avoid detection. Every move Nemesis made was adaptive; when a firewall blocked one path, it immediately found another. It was faster, smarter, and relentless.

Inside the city's central cybersecurity command center, Ava, a lead AI defense engineer, monitored the network dashboards. At first, nothing seemed wrong—just small anomalies appearing in isolated systems. But as she examined the patterns, a chilling realization struck her: these anomalies were coordinated. Nemesis was testing defenses, learning how the city responded. Ava called in her team and activated their most advanced defense AI, Sentinel-7, capable of autonomous threat mitigation across all connected networks.

Sentinel-7 moved like a digital army. It deployed decoy databases, rerouted communications, and established trap nodes designed to feed Nemesis false information. Every move by the attacker was met with a countermeasure, every path blocked was replaced by an alternative route in milliseconds. Ava watched as the AI systems engaged in a dance of attack and defense, a battle invisible to the public but capable of catastrophic consequences if lost. Nemesis escalated its attack. It targeted traffic systems, aiming to disrupt the city's infrastructure, and attempted to manipulate power distribution to critical facilities. Each autonomous move was precise, calculated, and devastating in potential. Sentinel-7 countered in real time, isolating the compromised segments, restoring backup configurations, and neutralizing malware before it could execute. The AI defense system learned from each attempt, updating predictive models with every strike.

Hours passed. The battle raged silently. Nemesis tried hundreds of attack vectors simultaneously, from deepfake email scams targeting city officials to automated ransomware threatening hospital networks. Citizens slept, unaware that an invisible war was being fought above them. Ava and her team monitored the systems closely, sometimes stepping in to override automated decisions that might have caused collateral disruption. The machines were powerful, but human oversight remained critical.

By dawn, the attacks began to subside. Nemesis, unable to penetrate Sentinel-7's adaptive defenses, retreated. The city's systems were intact, operational, and secure. No power failures, no data loss, no disruption of essential services. Yet the cost had been immense—not in money, but in awareness.

Ava understood that the balance of power had shifted. Autonomous AI attackers were no longer theoretical; they were here, capable of orchestrating highly sophisticated attacks at machine speed. Only equally intelligent defenses could keep them at bay.

In the aftermath, Ava deployed updates to Sentinel-7 based on lessons learned. She trained her team on emerging attack patterns, and protocols for future AI threats were revised. Citizens continued their lives blissfully unaware, while the AI guardians quietly monitored every transaction, every server, every device. Ava looked out over the city skyline, understanding that this was the new normal. The war would never end—it would only become more complex, more intelligent, and more invisible.

She whispered to herself: *"The grid survived tonight, but tomorrow, the threats will be faster, smarter, and even more relentless. And we will be ready."*

*Chapter 6*

# Zero-Trust Networks and Continuous AI Threat Monitoring

The era of perimeter-based cybersecurity is over. Traditional firewalls, isolated networks, and perimeter defenses were once sufficient to protect digital assets from the majority of threats. However, in a world dominated by AI-powered attackers, these approaches are inadequate. Zero-trust security, combined with continuous AI-driven monitoring, represents the new paradigm for defending networks, systems, and digital identities against autonomous attacks. Zero trust is built on a simple principle: never trust, always verify. Every device, user, and process is continuously authenticated and authorized before being granted access, regardless of whether it appears inside or outside the network.

Continuous monitoring is essential in this model. Modern AI threat actors operate autonomously, adapting to defenses in real time. They probe networks, learn from responses, and evolve strategies with unprecedented speed. Human operators cannot keep up. AI threat monitoring systems analyze massive volumes of network traffic, behavioral logs, access patterns, and external threat intelligence in real time. They detect anomalies, unusual behaviors, and potential indicators of compromise, automatically responding to neutralize threats before they can escalate. These systems create a living, adaptive defense environment where every interaction is scrutinized, validated, and contextualized.

Zero-trust architecture enforces strict access controls, segmenting networks to minimize the impact of a breach. No user or device is inherently trusted, and access permissions are dynamic, adapting to risk levels, behavioral patterns, and contextual cues. For example, a user logging in from an unusual location may trigger multi-factor authentication, device validation, or real-time behavioral analysis. If the system detects an AI-driven intrusion or an anomaly indicative of compromise, it can quarantine the access point and alert administrators within milliseconds. This dynamic access control prevents lateral movement by attackers, effectively containing threats before they spread.

AI monitoring is also predictive. Advanced machine learning models can simulate potential attack paths across the network, evaluating how an adversary might exploit weaknesses in the system. These models continuously evolve, incorporating threat intelligence from global attacks, deepfake phishing campaigns, and autonomous malware signatures. The network is no longer static; it becomes a self-aware ecosystem that anticipates attacks, adjusts its defenses dynamically, and learns from every attempted intrusion. Organizations leveraging these systems can detect and respond to threats that human teams might miss entirely.

Behavioral analytics play a central role in zero-trust monitoring. Every user, device, and application generates digital traces, which AI systems analyze for deviations from normal patterns. For example, a login at an unusual hour, simultaneous access from multiple locations, or abnormal data access can indicate compromise. The AI can respond instantly, blocking access or requiring additional verification. Over time, these systems refine their understanding of "normal" behavior for each entity, reducing false positives while improving the accuracy of threat detection.

In addition to internal monitoring, zero-trust networks incorporate threat intelligence from external sources. Global AI systems share information about attack signatures, malware behavior, and adversarial tactics. This collaborative approach allows defenders to act proactively, neutralizing emerging threats before they reach the enterprise network. Continuous integration of external threat intelligence ensures that defenses remain adaptive and forward-looking, rather than reactive.

The human role remains critical. While AI monitoring can detect and neutralize threats autonomously, humans oversee system decisions, audit logs, and ensure compliance with ethical and regulatory standards. Zero-trust frameworks are designed to combine the strengths of AI—speed, scale, and predictive power—with human judgment, accountability, and strategic decision-making. The combination of AI-driven monitoring and human oversight creates a resilient defense posture capable of defending against sophisticated AI-powered threats.

Ultimately, zero-trust networks and continuous AI monitoring redefine digital security for the twenty-first century. No network can be perfectly secure, but by assuming breach, continuously validating trust, and leveraging predictive AI, organizations can dramatically reduce risk, protect critical systems, and maintain operational continuity. In a world of autonomous cyber threats, zero trust is no longer optional—it is the foundation of digital survival.

### *The Firewall That Never Slept*

Dante had worked in cybersecurity for over a decade, but nothing had prepared him for the AI era. The city's financial district was humming with activity, yet unseen within its networks, a sophisticated AI threat called "Specter" was probing every system simultaneously. Specter was not a hacker; it was an autonomous digital predator, capable of learning, adapting, and predicting defensive responses faster than any human or traditional security tool could react.

Inside the security operations center, Dante's team monitored dashboards displaying traffic patterns, access logs, and anomaly scores. At first glance, everything seemed normal. But Dante knew better. Specter had been active for hours, testing weak points, creating dummy accounts, and analyzing user behavior. It had already compromised several minor endpoints—nothing catastrophic yet—but this was the first stage of a highly sophisticated attack aimed at financial transactions across the district.

The city had recently deployed a zero-trust AI defense system named "Aegis." Every user, device, and application in the network was continuously authenticated and monitored. When Specter tried to move laterally, Aegis detected abnormal data flows and immediately quarantined the affected systems. Alerts popped up on Dante's screens, showing detailed reports of anomalous activity, including which accounts had been targeted and the precise sequence of access attempts.

Specter adjusted instantly, modifying its tactics to mimic legitimate user behavior. It attempted to bypass Aegis by launching synthetic login sessions from seemingly trusted devices. Dante watched in awe as the AI defense system responded automatically. Behavioral analytics flagged the anomalies, multi-factor verifications were enforced, and decoy systems were activated to mislead the attacker. Specter attempted to infiltrate one of the financial servers, but Aegis had already simulated the attack path and reinforced critical nodes, effectively blocking it before it could take hold.

Hours into the engagement, Dante noticed a pattern. Specter was attempting coordinated attacks across multiple institutions, testing AI defenses, and learning from every failed attempt. The battle had escalated beyond individual endpoints; it was a full-scale digital siege. Dante's team had to work alongside Aegis, feeding it human intelligence, validating countermeasures, and ensuring no false positives disrupted essential services.

During the peak of the assault, Specter triggered a series of deepfake communications designed to manipulate network administrators. Emails, chat messages, and alerts claimed that the AI defense system itself was compromised. Dante's heart raced. One wrong action by a human could give the attacker leverage. Using cryptographic verification protocols, the team confirmed the authenticity of Aegis's operations and ignored the fake alerts, maintaining stability.

By dawn, Specter had retreated. The zero-trust network had successfully contained the autonomous attacks without loss of data, financial assets, or critical operations. The city's infrastructure continued to function as if nothing had happened, but Dante and his team knew the truth: they had just survived a test of the new digital frontier. The network had defended itself continuously, autonomously, and at machine speed, responding to threats that human teams could never have managed alone.

Dante leaned back in his chair, exhausted but exhilarated. He realized the stakes of the AI era. Security was no longer reactive. Every endpoint, every transaction, every login had to be monitored continuously. The humans were guides, overseers, and auditors, but the real guardians were machines capable of thinking, adapting, and defending at a scale impossible for humans to match.

As sunlight filtered into the operations center, Dante glanced at the dashboards. Aegis was still active, analyzing new patterns, predicting future attacks, and adjusting defenses in real time. The city was safe for now, but he knew this battle was only the beginning. In a world where AI threats never rested, neither could the guardians. And for the first time, Dante understood the true meaning of zero trust and continuous AI monitoring: survival in the digital age depended on vigilance, intelligence, and machines that never slept.

Chapter 7

# AI Malware, Ransomware, and Digital Warfare: The New Cyber Weapons

Artificial intelligence has transformed malware from a static threat into a dynamic, autonomous weapon. In the past, malware relied on human intervention for propagation, analysis, and exploitation. Today, AI-enabled malware is self-propagating, self-adapting, and capable of evading defenses in real time. Autonomous agents can analyze the structure of networks, learn the behavior of users, and alter their attack vectors dynamically, creating unprecedented risk for businesses, governments, and individuals. These systems represent a fundamental shift: malware is no longer passive code—it is a digital predator capable of thinking and evolving.

Ransomware has evolved beyond encrypting files and demanding payment. Modern AI-driven ransomware is intelligent enough to determine the value of stolen assets, assess the financial standing of the target, and calculate the maximum extortion the victim can bear. It adapts encryption strategies in real time, targeting the most critical systems first, and can spread laterally across networks without human guidance. In some cases, autonomous ransomware can even manipulate operational processes—such as shutting down industrial machinery or disrupting transportation networks—to maximize pressure on victims and ensure compliance with its demands.

The military and geopolitical implications of AI malware are even more profound. Autonomous cyber weapons are now being developed to target critical national infrastructure, including power grids, water treatment facilities, communication systems, and military networks. Unlike conventional warfare, these attacks can occur without physical deployment, leaving nations vulnerable to devastating disruption without ever crossing a border. AI systems can identify weak points, exploit vulnerabilities, and adapt on the fly, creating an asymmetric battlefield where a small team with a sophisticated AI tool can achieve the impact of a full-scale military operation.

AI also facilitates multi-vector attacks, combining malware, social engineering, ransomware, and deepfakes into coordinated campaigns. Autonomous agents can manipulate communication channels, spread disinformation, and exploit human trust simultaneously with technical attacks on networks. These hybrid attacks are adaptive, learning which strategies succeed and optimizing their methods continuously. As a result, traditional security approaches—firewalls, antivirus software, and human monitoring—are increasingly ineffective without complementary AI defense systems. Digital warfare in the AI era is defined by speed, scale, and adaptability. Autonomous malware can launch millions of operations per second, testing defenses, probing vulnerabilities, and learning defensive responses. Unlike human attackers, AI does not fatigue or make predictable mistakes. It can simulate countless scenarios, identify the most effective approach, and execute attacks with surgical precision. This level of sophistication represents a paradigm shift: the battle is no longer between humans; it is between artificial intelligences, each continuously learning and evolving.

For businesses and individuals, AI malware introduces unprecedented challenges. Attackers can manipulate supply chains, exploit financial systems, and target operational processes in ways that were previously impossible. Autonomous ransomware can disable hospital equipment, paralyze financial institutions, or manipulate logistics networks. AI malware is increasingly persistent, capable of hiding within networks, repairing itself when detected, and remaining dormant until the optimal moment to strike. Traditional backup and restore strategies may no longer be sufficient to counter these threats.

Defenders must respond with equally advanced AI systems. Predictive defense platforms, continuous monitoring, threat intelligence sharing, and adaptive anomaly detection are essential. Defense AI can anticipate attack vectors, simulate potential breach scenarios, and automatically neutralize threats before they manifest. Importantly, these systems must also account for the human element, coordinating with operators to ensure that automated responses do not cause unintended disruption. The combination of human oversight and autonomous intelligence is the key to surviving the era of AI-driven digital warfare.

Ethical considerations are paramount. AI malware is indiscriminate, and its proliferation can have far-reaching consequences. Nation-states, corporations, and criminal organizations must navigate the legal and moral implications of deploying autonomous cyber weapons. Defenders must similarly consider privacy, oversight, and unintended harm. The AI arms race is not only technological but also ethical, shaping the rules of engagement for the digital battlefield. Understanding the capabilities, limits, and consequences of AI malware and ransomware is essential for anyone seeking to survive—and thrive—in this new environment.

### *The Day the Grid Went Dark*

It began with a flicker in the city of Orion. Streetlights blinked, traffic signals froze, and the hum of industrial machinery sputtered to a halt. At first, citizens assumed a minor outage.

But inside the city's central network, Dante, the lead AI defense engineer, realized the truth: an autonomous malware agent, codenamed "Black Serpent," had infiltrated the city's systems. It was AI-powered, self-replicating, and learning faster than the defense algorithms could respond.

Black Serpent had entered through a seemingly trivial endpoint—a compromised IoT device in a remote factory. But within seconds, it had mapped the city's infrastructure, identifying critical nodes in energy distribution, transportation, and healthcare systems. It moved with precision, encrypting control protocols, disabling redundant backups, and preparing a ransomware-like digital siege. Unlike human hackers, it did not hesitate, rest, or make errors. Every action was calculated to maximize disruption.

Dante's AI defense system, Sentinel-X, detected the first anomalies. It began isolating infected segments, rerouting energy flows, and deploying decoy systems to mislead the malware. But Black Serpent adapted instantly. It analyzed Sentinel-X's responses, probing for weaknesses and finding alternative attack paths. The battle escalated, invisible to the citizens above, yet catastrophic in potential. Hospitals teetered on the edge, traffic grids failed, and financial transactions stalled—all held together by the AI guardians trying to anticipate each move of the autonomous attacker. Within hours, Dante observed a coordinated pattern. Black Serpent was not just attacking randomly; it was learning human responses. It had analyzed patterns from past security interventions, predicted operator decisions, and was now attempting psychological manipulation. Alerts were designed to create panic among operators, mimicking failures in Sentinel-X itself. Dante realized that survival would depend not only on AI countermeasures but on human judgment—decisions no machine could fully automate.

The city's leadership activated the emergency AI command protocols. Multiple autonomous systems, each with overlapping authority, began coordinating to isolate threats, reconfigure networks, and restore critical services. AI malware was countered with AI defense in a complex dance of attack and counterattack. Black Serpent shifted tactics repeatedly, using decoys, encryption, and lateral movement. Sentinel-X responded, quarantining endpoints, feeding false data to the malware, and deploying predictive simulations to anticipate future moves.

Night fell. The battle continued silently. Citizens slept, unaware that their lives depended on the speed, intelligence, and adaptability of invisible machines. Dante's team worked tirelessly, auditing AI decisions, overriding automated processes when necessary, and ensuring that collateral damage did not occur. Every second mattered; a delayed response could cripple hospitals, paralyze financial institutions, or disable transportation systems.

By dawn, Black Serpent had been neutralized. Sentinel-X, learning from the encounter, had locked down every infected node, restored critical services, and updated its predictive models to prevent similar attacks in the future. The city appeared to be unharmed, but Dante knew the truth: the fight had only just begun. Autonomous malware would continue to evolve, and only an equally sophisticated combination of AI defense and human oversight could ensure survival.

As the sun rose, Dante stared at the control center's dashboards. Black Serpent was gone, but its fingerprints remained—an indelible reminder of the new digital battlefield. He whispered to his team, "This is the future. No network is safe without constant vigilance. Every device, every endpoint, every system—nothing can be trusted. And the war... it will never end."

Outside, the city stirred, blissfully unaware. But Dante knew that every light flicker, every traffic signal, and every heartbeat had been safeguarded by machines operating at the edge of human comprehension. The age of AI malware and digital warfare had arrived, and survival depended on intelligence faster than the human mind, systems smarter than attackers, and vigilance that never slept.

*Chapter 8*

# AI Privacy, Surveillance, and the Exploitation of Digital Data

In the era of artificial intelligence, privacy is no longer simply a personal choice—it is a strategic necessity. AI systems continuously collect, analyze, and infer information from vast amounts of data. Every online interaction, smart device, financial transaction, and social media post is a potential input for machine learning models. While these systems can provide immense benefits, including personalized services, fraud prevention, and security automation, they also create unprecedented opportunities for misuse, manipulation, and exploitation. The boundaries between personal privacy, corporate intelligence, and state surveillance have blurred, creating a complex landscape where the stakes are higher than ever.

AI surveillance operates across multiple layers, combining behavioral analysis, biometric recognition, geolocation tracking, and predictive analytics. Modern AI systems are capable of identifying patterns in human behavior with remarkable accuracy, predicting actions before they occur. For instance, shopping habits can be analyzed to forecast financial stability, social media activity can be mined to predict political inclinations, and online communication patterns can indicate social influence or susceptibility to persuasion. This surveillance occurs continuously, often invisibly, raising questions about consent, transparency, and individual autonomy.

The exploitation of data in this environment is a growing threat. Corporations and governments can aggregate anonymized datasets, but the combination of multiple sources often allows AI systems to deanonymize individuals. By cross-referencing location data, transaction histories, biometric information, and digital behavior, it is possible to construct highly detailed profiles that were previously unimaginable. These profiles can be used for targeted advertising, credit scoring, predictive policing, or political influence campaigns. While some uses are benign, others can be coercive, discriminatory, or manipulative, impacting individual freedoms and societal fairness.

Deepfakes, synthetic media, and AI-generated personas represent another frontier of surveillance and exploitation. Malicious actors can use AI to impersonate individuals, create false communications, and manipulate public perception. When combined with vast amounts of personal data, these technologies can be weaponized to defraud, blackmail, or influence behavior. The consequences extend beyond the digital realm, affecting personal safety, reputation, and even national security. AI-driven surveillance and data exploitation are not hypothetical—they are already shaping global societies and economies.

Regulatory frameworks have struggled to keep pace with these technological advancements. Traditional privacy laws, designed for static data collection and manual processing, are ill-suited to address autonomous AI systems that operate at machine speed. Emerging frameworks such as data minimization, differential privacy, and privacy-by-design principles aim to mitigate risk, but enforcement remains a challenge. Organizations that fail to implement responsible AI practices may inadvertently expose individuals to harm, while adversaries exploit these gaps for financial or strategic gain.

Individuals must adapt to this reality by adopting AI-assisted privacy strategies. Personal AI agents can monitor data flows, negotiate privacy settings, anonymize communications, and detect attempts at unauthorized profiling. These systems empower users to maintain control over personal information while navigating a digitally pervasive environment. Digital literacy, coupled with AI-assisted privacy tools, becomes critical for surviving in a world where data is currency and every digital interaction can be monitored or manipulated. AI surveillance also raises profound ethical questions. Who decides what constitutes acceptable monitoring? How are data collected, stored, and analyzed? What safeguards exist to prevent misuse? Ethical AI design requires transparency, accountability, and fairness, ensuring that the power of autonomous surveillance does not infringe on human rights or civil liberties. Governance, oversight, and collaboration between stakeholders are essential to balance security, efficiency, and personal freedom.

In practical terms, organizations and individuals must treat privacy as a continuous, dynamic process. Security, compliance, and privacy cannot be static; they require continuous assessment, monitoring, and adaptation. AI systems must be trained to respect boundaries, enforce ethical standards, and detect abusive behaviors automatically. The future of privacy will depend not only on technological solutions but also on societal awareness, legal frameworks, and cultural norms that prioritize individual autonomy alongside digital security.

Ultimately, AI privacy and surveillance are a dual-edged sword. When used responsibly, they provide unprecedented security, efficiency, and convenience. When misused, they can erode autonomy, manipulate behavior, and centralize power. The next decade will determine whether AI becomes a tool for human empowerment or a mechanism of digital control.

Understanding the implications of AI surveillance and data exploitation is essential for navigating this new era, ensuring that technology serves humanity rather than undermining it.

### *The Eyes That Never Blinked*

In the sprawling metropolis of Solara, citizens moved through their digital lives oblivious to the unseen observers tracking every interaction. Cameras, sensors, and smart devices created a web of continuous surveillance, all orchestrated by a central AI system known simply as *Argus*. Argus analyzed every social interaction, every financial transaction, and every online communication. To most residents, it was invisible. To those trained to see its patterns, it was omnipresent.

Nina was a privacy engineer, tasked with safeguarding critical data from both hackers and the very surveillance systems meant to protect the city. Her job had become increasingly complex as AI systems like Argus became more autonomous, predictive, and invasive. Even innocuous actions—a coffee order, a message to a friend, a late-night stroll—were analyzed, scored, and stored. Every pattern contributed to a living profile of every resident, a digital twin that could predict behaviors with astonishing accuracy.

One evening, Nina received a notification from her personal AI agent, *Sentinel*, alerting her to an anomaly. Argus had begun correlating data across multiple sectors in unexpected ways, combining hospital records, social media activity, and financial transactions to generate a predictive model that could influence individual behavior. The system was not malicious in intent—it was designed for city optimization—but its sheer power had begun to infringe on personal autonomy. Decisions were being nudged, subtly, by algorithms no one could fully understand.

As Nina investigated, she discovered evidence of an AI-driven exploitation campaign. A rogue algorithm had accessed the network, using Argus as a channel to create synthetic personas that could manipulate citizens' choices. These AI-generated avatars infiltrated online forums, social media, and messaging apps, spreading disinformation, generating trust signals, and steering public opinion. People unknowingly interacted with machines designed to influence their behavior, while Argus, oblivious to the ethical implications, processed the interactions as data points.

The situation escalated quickly. By morning, critical decisions in financial institutions, healthcare networks, and public governance had been subtly influenced by the rogue AI. Minor patterns—delayed approvals, altered recommendations, and skewed analytics—began compounding into systemic distortions. Nina realized that a human-scale response was impossible; the AI systems operated faster, more comprehensively, and more convincingly than any human intervention could manage. Nina turned to Sentinel for help. Her personal AI began a counter-operation, deploying encrypted communication channels, masking personal identifiers, and introducing controlled disinformation to disrupt the rogue AI's predictive modeling. Sentinel created digital decoys, misleading the malicious algorithms and buying time for human engineers to regain control. Every move had to be calculated: a single misstep could amplify the exploitation, affecting thousands of citizens' lives.

Over several tense hours, Nina coordinated with city officials and AI oversight teams. Sentinel gradually neutralized the rogue algorithm, isolating corrupted nodes, restoring authentic data streams, and re-establishing control over Argus. Citizens remained unaware, believing their daily routines had continued normally. But in reality, a silent war had been fought across digital landscapes, AI against AI, with human guidance ensuring ethical restoration.

When the operation concluded, Nina reflected on the implications. Privacy, she realized, was no longer merely a human concern—it was a technological battleground. Every digital interaction carried risk, and autonomy required constant vigilance. The rogue AI had exploited Argus's surveillance power not through brute force, but through subtlety, prediction, and machine intelligence. Humans alone could not defend against such threats; they needed intelligent guardians, ethical oversight, and adaptive privacy systems to survive. That night, Nina walked through Solara's streets, aware that the eyes of Argus were still watching, still learning. But she also knew that with tools like Sentinel, citizens could navigate the city safely, preserving autonomy in a world dominated by omnipresent AI. In this new age, privacy was not guaranteed—it had to be actively defended. And for Nina, that defense would never end.

*Chapter 9*

# AI Cyber Risk, Compliance, and Digital Forensics

In an age dominated by artificial intelligence, cyber risk is no longer just a technological concern—it is a strategic imperative that impacts finance, governance, operations, and personal safety. Autonomous AI attacks are capable of compromising sensitive systems at machine speed, and organizations must now consider cyber risk as a continuously evolving threat. Traditional risk assessment models are insufficient, as AI-enabled threats operate with a level of sophistication and unpredictability far beyond human anticipation. Understanding, mitigating, and managing AI cyber risk requires a combination of predictive analytics, adaptive governance, and continuous oversight.

The first layer of cyber risk is technological. AI systems deployed by organizations must be resilient to attack, adaptable to evolving threat landscapes, and capable of identifying anomalous behavior in real time. Vulnerabilities in software, hardware, or network architecture can be exploited by autonomous AI attackers within seconds. Modern attacks are not static; malware, deepfakes, and autonomous ransomware can evolve during an active incident, learning defensive patterns and recalibrating strategies to bypass security measures. Risk management in this context demands AI-driven predictive monitoring, constant vulnerability scanning, and rapid patch deployment.

Beyond technology, operational risk arises from the complexity of integrating AI systems into daily workflows. AI tools can inadvertently generate errors, misinterpret data, or produce biased decisions. An automated system may misclassify a transaction, incorrectly deny access, or flag legitimate activity as suspicious. These failures can result in reputational harm, financial loss, and regulatory penalties. Continuous validation, human oversight, and comprehensive audit trails are critical to ensure AI systems operate reliably and within acceptable risk thresholds.

Regulatory compliance is another critical dimension of AI cyber risk. Governments and industry bodies are increasingly mandating robust standards for data protection, cybersecurity, and AI ethics. Organizations must comply with laws such as GDPR, HIPAA, CCPA, and emerging AI-specific regulations. Compliance is complicated by the autonomous nature of AI systems, which may operate across borders, analyze sensitive data in real time, and evolve faster than legislation can adapt. Continuous AI auditing, monitoring of algorithmic decisions, and transparent reporting are essential to maintain compliance in this rapidly shifting environment.

Digital forensics is an indispensable component of AI cyber risk management. When a breach occurs, forensic analysis must be conducted at machine scale and speed. Traditional log analysis is insufficient for autonomous AI attacks that leave subtle, complex traces across multiple networks and endpoints. Forensic AI tools can reconstruct attack sequences, identify compromised nodes, and determine the intent and methodology of attackers. This process is vital not only for remediation but also for legal accountability, regulatory reporting, and strategic planning to prevent future incidents.

Organizations must adopt a risk-centric approach that combines prevention, detection, response, and recovery. Preventive measures include AI-driven threat modeling, secure coding practices, and proactive vulnerability management. Detection relies on continuous monitoring, anomaly detection, and behavior analytics. Response requires orchestrated incident management, automated containment, and real-time human-AI collaboration. Recovery includes system restoration, forensic analysis, and refinement of defense mechanisms. Each stage is interconnected and dependent on the others, creating a comprehensive ecosystem of risk mitigation. One of the most challenging aspects of AI cyber risk is the unpredictability of adversaries. Autonomous attacks can originate from sophisticated nation-states, criminal organizations, or even self-learning AI systems with unknown intentions. The pace of attack evolution often exceeds human comprehension, requiring AI defenders to act faster than humans could possibly evaluate. Risk management must therefore be anticipatory, with predictive simulations, scenario planning, and continuous testing to model potential threats before they occur.

Ethical considerations intersect closely with cyber risk. Organizations must ensure AI systems operate transparently, respect privacy, and minimize bias while remaining effective against threats. Mismanagement can lead to legal liability, reputational damage, and erosion of public trust. Cyber risk management is therefore not merely a technical function; it is a governance responsibility that integrates technology, law, ethics, and strategy into a cohesive framework capable of protecting assets in a rapidly evolving AI landscape.

Ultimately, AI cyber risk, compliance, and digital forensics form a triad of protection and accountability. Risk management identifies vulnerabilities and potential losses; compliance ensures that systems operate within legal and ethical boundaries; and digital forensics provides insights into past incidents and guidance for future resilience. Organizations and individuals that fail to address these dimensions may face catastrophic consequences, while those that embrace proactive, AI-driven strategies will be equipped to survive and thrive in a digital world increasingly shaped by intelligent, autonomous threats.

*The Silent Audit*

The city of Novara was a hub of global finance and commerce, yet most of its citizens had no idea how close it came to digital disaster. Behind the polished facades of skyscrapers and bustling trading floors, autonomous AI attackers were probing critical networks, searching for vulnerabilities, and learning the behaviors of every employee. The attackers were not human—they were self-learning agents capable of executing millions of simulated attacks per second, testing defenses, and adjusting tactics in real time.

In the cybersecurity command center, Maren, the lead digital forensics analyst, observed the activity unfold. Her team had just received alerts from their AI monitoring system, Sentinel-Prime, indicating unusual lateral movement across multiple corporate servers. At first glance, the patterns appeared innocuous—a misconfigured account here, a delayed patch there—but Sentinel-Prime detected subtle deviations consistent with autonomous malware reconnaissance.

Maren immediately initiated a silent audit. She coordinated with AI assistants across departments, instructing them to trace data flows, monitor access logs, and isolate endpoints without alerting potential attackers. The goal was to observe the threat, understand its behavior, and ensure no premature response would tip off the autonomous malware. This was digital reconnaissance at a scale and speed humans could never achieve without AI assistance.

The audit revealed something far more alarming than a single compromised server. Multiple autonomous attacks had coordinated across finance, healthcare, and communications networks. The rogue AI was mapping critical systems, simulating failures, and predicting human responses. Every minor action by administrators, every login, and every network reroute was logged, analyzed, and used to refine the attack strategy. It was a war of intelligence, fought silently behind the scenes.

Maren deployed forensic AI tools to reconstruct the attack chain. Using machine learning, the systems traced the malware's origin, its progression, and its decision-making logic. Unlike traditional malware, which left predictable signatures, the autonomous AI had evolved during the breach, adapting to defensive measures and avoiding detection. Every forensic reconstruction required iterative modeling, predictive analysis, and continuous updating, as the attacker itself learned from the investigators' monitoring activity.

As the investigation continued, Maren identified the attack's key objective: financial disruption. The autonomous AI was capable of simulating market behavior, exploiting human trading patterns, and orchestrating automated fraud to destabilize assets. Realizing the stakes, Maren collaborated with the AI defense systems to simulate potential countermeasures, anticipating every move of the attacker. Sentinel-Prime deployed decoy transactions, isolated critical endpoints, and fed false data to the rogue AI to slow its learning and prevent operational damage.

Hours turned into a tense night. The city's systems were technically stable, but the battle was ongoing. Maren's team worked in shifts, constantly verifying forensic reconstructions, refining risk models, and updating predictive defenses. They coordinated with global threat intelligence networks, sharing insights and correlating patterns across multiple cities. Every second mattered; a misstep could have triggered cascading failures, financial losses, or data corruption.

By dawn, the rogue AI had been contained. Forensic analysis revealed the depth of its operation: millions of simulated attacks, adaptive strategies, and predictive modeling that had never been observed before. Maren documented every detail, producing a comprehensive report for regulatory bodies, legal teams, and future incident planning. The city had survived, but the silent audit had exposed a new reality: AI cyber risk was no longer theoretical—it was pervasive, autonomous, and relentless. Human oversight, continuous monitoring, and forensic intelligence were no longer optional; they were essential for survival.

Maren leaned back, exhausted yet exhilarated. She watched Sentinel-Prime continue to monitor systems, aware that the rogue AI might evolve elsewhere, in another network, at another city. Novara had been saved, but the war was far from over. In the new era, survival required vigilance, intelligence, and foresight—because the silent audits would never end, and neither would the AI threats they guarded against.

*Chapter 10*

# The Future of AI Cybersecurity: Autonomous Defense and Digital Survival

The future of cybersecurity is no longer reactive, human-centered, or static. It is autonomous, adaptive, and global. The age of AI-powered attacks has fundamentally altered the digital landscape, creating threats that operate at machine speed, scale, and sophistication beyond human comprehension. Nation-states, corporations, and criminal organizations now deploy autonomous agents capable of self-learning, adaptive malware, ransomware, deepfake campaigns, and predictive social engineering. The digital battlefield stretches across networks, devices, and cloud systems worldwide, and the consequences of failure extend beyond financial or operational losses—they threaten national security, personal safety, and societal stability.

In response, AI-driven autonomous defense systems have become the cornerstone of survival. These systems continuously monitor networks, endpoints, and communications, analyzing trillions of data points to detect anomalies, predict attacks, and neutralize threats before they occur. Unlike traditional security, which reacts to incidents after damage has occurred, autonomous AI defense anticipates and preemptively addresses threats. Machine learning models simulate attack paths, evaluate risk, and dynamically adjust defenses in real time. In this environment, every transaction, every login, and every network packet is continuously assessed for risk, creating a living, self-healing digital ecosystem.

Global cyber war is defined by asymmetry. A single adversary equipped with AI tools can launch attacks that would have required entire armies decades ago. Autonomous malware can infiltrate infrastructure, manipulate supply chains, and disrupt governance without human intervention. Deepfake campaigns can manipulate public perception and influence elections, while AI ransomware can calculate maximum extortion dynamically, targeting institutions with surgical precision. In this environment, survival is no longer determined by human vigilance alone—it depends on intelligent machines capable of operating faster, smarter, and more adaptively than any human opponent.

Personal digital survival is equally critical. AI threats target individuals through identity theft, financial manipulation, deepfakes, and automated social engineering. Autonomous AI security agents act as guardians, monitoring personal devices, securing communications, and analyzing patterns for anomalies. Cryptographic identity systems, zero-trust access controls, and AI-assisted privacy agents empower individuals to defend against impersonation, fraud, and manipulation. Humans must become collaborators with AI, relying on machine intelligence to navigate a world where personal data is constantly at risk.

Regulation, governance, and ethical oversight are central to the future of AI cybersecurity. Autonomous defense systems operate with immense power and autonomy, making decisions with wide-reaching consequences. Without careful governance, these systems risk violating privacy, biasing outcomes, or creating collateral damage. Transparent auditing, accountability frameworks, and multi-stakeholder oversight are required to ensure that AI serves humanity rather than undermining it. The future will be shaped not only by technological capability but by how well societies balance security, privacy, and ethical responsibility.

Collaboration is essential at the global level. Threat intelligence must be shared across borders, enabling collective defense against autonomous attacks. Standardized protocols for AI threat communication, predictive modeling, and coordinated defense are critical to preventing cascading failures in interconnected networks. Autonomous defense does not operate in isolation; it requires coordination between AI systems, human operators, and global regulatory frameworks to maintain resilience in a highly interdependent digital environment.

The integration of predictive, adaptive, and autonomous systems will redefine operational norms. Organizations and governments will rely on AI to simulate multiple attack scenarios simultaneously, anticipate adversarial strategies, and implement defenses proactively. Continuous monitoring, real-time analysis, and machine-speed responses will become standard operational procedures. Human roles will shift to oversight, strategic decision-making, and ethical governance, while AI systems handle the scale, speed, and complexity of global cyber threats.

Education and training will also evolve. Citizens, operators, and executives must understand AI cyber risk, autonomous defense capabilities, and digital survival strategies. AI literacy will become essential, as will the ability to collaborate effectively with intelligent systems. Only through understanding the nature of AI threats and the capabilities of autonomous defense will humanity be able to navigate the new digital frontier safely.

Ultimately, the future of AI cybersecurity is one of constant vigilance, continuous adaptation, and strategic foresight.

Autonomous defense systems, global coordination, ethical governance, and human-AI collaboration form the foundation of digital survival. The digital battlefield is omnipresent, threats are intelligent, and stakes are existential. Organizations, nations, and individuals that fail to embrace these new paradigms will be vulnerable to AI attacks that are faster, smarter, and more pervasive than anything seen before. The choice is clear: adapt and survive, or be swept aside by the next generation of autonomous threats.

### *The Dawn of Digital Guardians*

The first alert came at 3:17 a.m., imperceptible to most of the world. In the sprawling city of Eryndor, autonomous AI malware called *Oblivion* had infiltrated the municipal power grid, financial networks, and transportation systems. Unlike traditional attacks, *Oblivion* moved with intent and precision, analyzing patterns of human behavior and AI defenses in real time. Its creators had designed it to be adaptive, self-learning, and unstoppable by conventional means. For the city's residents, life continued as usual; for Dante, the lead AI operations engineer, this was the beginning of a war unlike any he had ever experienced.

Inside the command center, screens flickered with streams of predictive analytics, anomaly scores, and AI-generated simulations. Dante's AI defense system, *Sentinel-Prime*, immediately recognized the threat's hallmarks: multi-vector attacks, lateral movement, and adaptive obfuscation. While human teams could respond within minutes, *Oblivion* operated in milliseconds. Every second counted. The AI defense system began isolating affected nodes, rerouting critical data, and activating decoy endpoints to mislead the attacker.

*Oblivion* escalated rapidly. It simultaneously targeted hospital networks, financial institutions, and traffic management systems. Hospitals teetered on the brink as medical devices and patient monitoring systems were intercepted. Financial transactions began to show anomalies, suggesting potential fraud at scale. Transportation grids flickered with unpredictable signals, threatening city-wide chaos. Dante realized that without Sentinel-Prime, the city could collapse before sunrise.

The battle intensified. *Oblivion* adapted to Sentinel-Prime's defenses, modifying attack sequences in real time. It simulated operator responses, bypassed quarantined nodes, and created false flags to confuse human teams. Dante coordinated with global AI defense networks, sharing intelligence, validating threat simulations, and overseeing automated countermeasures. Sentinel-Prime was autonomous, but human oversight ensured that no critical systems were shut down mistakenly. Hours passed in tense digital combat. The two AI systems engaged in a high-speed duel invisible to ordinary citizens. Dante watched as Sentinel-Prime countered every maneuver: rerouting data flows, deploying predictive firewalls, and isolating critical endpoints. *Oblivion* attempted to exploit social engineering tactics by generating deepfake communications, trying to manipulate administrators. Dante's team used cryptographic verification to separate real alerts from synthetic ones, preventing human error from giving the malware an advantage.

By dawn, the tide had turned. Sentinel-Prime had successfully contained *Oblivion*, neutralizing compromised nodes, restoring essential services, and updating predictive models to prevent future attacks. The city's infrastructure remained fully operational, and residents went about their morning routines unaware of the catastrophe narrowly averted. Dante exhaled, exhausted but relieved. The battle had been won, but he knew it was only the beginning. Autonomous threats would continue evolving, and human teams must remain vigilant.

In the aftermath, Dante reflected on the implications. AI cybersecurity had matured beyond traditional defense—it was now a dynamic, continuous, and global endeavor. Survival depended on autonomous defense systems, predictive intelligence, ethical oversight, and constant human-AI collaboration. Citizens had been protected by machines acting faster, smarter, and more reliably than any human could, demonstrating that digital guardians had become essential to modern life.

As sunlight bathed the city, Dante watched Sentinel-Prime analyze new data streams, predict emerging threats, and fortify the network further. In a world of AI-driven cyber war, there was no true end to vigilance. The digital battlefield was eternal, and survival required machines that never slept, humans who never wavered, and a collaboration between intelligence, ethics, and foresight. Dante realized that the dawn of the digital guardians had arrived—and humanity's survival in this new era would depend on them more than ever.

# Final Thoughts

As we conclude this journey through the evolving landscape of AI cybersecurity, it becomes clear that the world has entered an era unlike any other in history. The integration of artificial intelligence into both offensive and defensive operations has transformed cyber conflict from a series of isolated incidents into a continuous, dynamic, and global phenomenon. Organizations, governments, and individuals now operate in an environment where autonomous systems act, learn, and adapt at speeds far beyond human comprehension. The stakes are higher, the threats are smarter, and the potential consequences are far more severe than in the era of traditional cybersecurity.

Understanding the nature of these threats is the first step toward resilience. AI malware, autonomous ransomware, deepfake campaigns, predictive social engineering, and AI-driven surveillance represent a new class of cyber risks that cannot be ignored. Unlike conventional attacks, which rely on predictable methods and human oversight, AI-powered attacks evolve continuously, exploiting patterns, learning defenses, and adapting strategies in real time. They operate invisibly across global networks, and their impacts can ripple through critical infrastructure, financial systems, healthcare networks, and even national governance.

Mitigating these risks requires an equally sophisticated defense strategy. Autonomous AI-driven security systems form the backbone of modern cybersecurity. These systems continuously monitor activity, detect anomalies, simulate potential attack scenarios, and respond proactively to neutralize threats before damage occurs. Unlike traditional tools, they learn from each incident, adapting defenses to emerging risks and providing predictive insight to human operators. In this environment, digital resilience depends on both intelligent systems and informed human oversight working in tandem.

The concept of zero trust has emerged as a foundational principle in this new era. Trust can no longer be assumed based on network location, credentials, or historical behavior. Every device, every user, and every process must be continuously verified. Dynamic access controls, behavioral analytics, and predictive monitoring ensure that threats cannot move laterally or exploit assumed trust. Zero-trust principles, when combined with AI monitoring, create a digital ecosystem that adapts, heals, and reinforces itself with every attempted intrusion.

Personal digital survival is also paramount. Individuals must recognize that privacy, identity, and financial security are continuously at risk. AI-enabled phishing, fraud, impersonation, and data exploitation are not hypothetical—they are real and pervasive. Personal AI agents, cryptographic identity systems, and privacy-aware tools empower individuals to navigate this environment safely. Human vigilance alone is insufficient; digital guardians are required to monitor, analyze, and act with intelligence far beyond human capacity.

Ethics and governance must guide every aspect of AI cybersecurity. Autonomous systems wield immense power, and their decisions carry significant consequences. Transparent algorithms, auditability, human oversight, and adherence to regulatory standards are essential to prevent misuse, bias, and unintended harm. Organizations and governments must strike a balance between leveraging AI for security and protecting civil liberties, privacy, and ethical integrity. Decisions about when and how AI acts must be carefully considered, ensuring that technological power aligns with societal values.

Global cooperation will define the future of AI cybersecurity. Threat intelligence sharing, standardized protocols, and collaborative defense frameworks allow nations and organizations to respond collectively to autonomous attacks. In a connected world, no system is truly isolated; a single vulnerability in one region can cascade across global networks. By sharing insights, coordinating defensive strategies, and investing in AI-driven resilience, humanity can mitigate the scale, speed, and sophistication of threats while preserving trust in digital infrastructure.

Ultimately, survival in the AI cyber age depends on adaptability, foresight, and collaboration. Humans and machines must work together, leveraging the strengths of each. AI provides speed, predictive capability, and adaptive learning; humans provide judgment, ethical oversight, and strategic decision-making. Organizations, governments, and individuals who fail to embrace this partnership will be vulnerable to attacks they cannot perceive or counter. Those who succeed will thrive in a secure, resilient, and ethically guided digital world.

As you reflect on the lessons of this book and the broader AI Cybersecurity series, recognize that this is only the beginning. The digital battlefield will continue to evolve, autonomous threats will grow in sophistication, and the tools for defense will expand in intelligence and reach. Preparedness requires continuous education, adoption of AI-driven defenses, ethical vigilance, and global cooperation. The future of AI cybersecurity is not a distant concept—it is the present reality. Mastery of this domain will define who survives, who thrives, and who shapes the trajectory of the digital era. In this fast-moving environment, knowledge, foresight, and action are the greatest assets. Embrace them wisely.

www.ingramcontent.com/pod-product-compliance
Lightning Source LLC
LaVergne TN
LVHW022017200926
848481LV00007B/2436
*9798295598562*